SO YOU WANNA BE

In a

BAND

MICHELLE GARCIA ANDERSEN

Rourke
Educational Media
rourkeeducationalmedia.com

Before Reading:

Building Academic Vocabulary and Background Knowledge

Before reading a book, it is important to tap into what your child or students already know about the topic. This will help them develop their vocabulary, increase their reading comprehension, and make connections across the curriculum.

1. *Look at the cover of the book. What will this book be about?*
2. *What do you already know about the topic?*
3. *Let's study the Table of Contents. What will you learn about in the book's chapters?*
4. *What would you like to learn about this topic? Do you think you might learn about it from this book? Why or why not?*
5. *Use a reading journal to write about your knowledge of this topic. Record what you already know about the topic and what you hope to learn about the topic.*
6. *Read the book.*
7. *In your reading journal, record what you learned about the topic and your response to the book.*
8. *After reading the book complete the activities below.*

Content Area Vocabulary

Read the list. What do these words mean?

auditions
complementary
consequences
consume
debut
distribute
luxury
maintain
resolving
various

After Reading:

Comprehension and Extension Activity

After reading the book, work on the following questions with your child or students in order to check their level of reading comprehension and content mastery.

1. *What happens at auditions? (Summarize)*
2. *What are some other things not mentioned in the book you might want to think about before joining or starting a band? (Infer)*
3. *How does a band get its music to an audience? (Asking Questions)*
4. *What is your favorite band? What do you like about them? (Text to Self Connection)*
5. *What are some good places for new bands to play? (Asking Questions)*

Extension Activity

Make a list of your favorite bands. Think about why you enjoy their music. Have you ever seen them play a live set, either in person or on TV? What was it like? Reflect on what is appealing about these bands. Are there things you can learn from them? Do they have a style you can build on to make your own? Write your ideas in a journal. Continue to add your thoughts about your own music and goals to this journal.

TABLE OF CONTENTS

Starting Your Own Band 4

Rules and Roles 8

Joining a Band 10

Time to Take It on the Road 11

Ready, Set, Record 16

Increasing Your Fan Base 18

Career Options 22

Glossary 30

Index 31

Show What You Know 31

Further Reading 31

About the Author 32

STARTING YOUR OWN BAND

Many people dream of being in a band. Some envision bright lights and screaming fans, while others simply want to jam. Whether you are interested in making music as a career or a hobby, some things remain the same. If you want to be in a band, you need to love music, be willing to work hard, and **maintain** a positive attitude.

THINK ABOUT IT

It's possible that not all of your friends are equally skilled musicians. Sometimes spending too much time together can get annoying. What if one of your friends decides to quit the band? If you form a band with friends, you'll need to know how to handle these issues.

When forming a band, it's important everyone gets along because you will be spending a lot of time together. If you're thinking of starting a band with your closest friends, consider the **consequences** of having your best friends as your bandmates.

One of the best ways to find band members is by holding an **audition**. This allows you and the people auditioning to see if your talents are **complementary**. It's important to be realistic about your abilities. It's okay to admit that you are a beginner. Remember, everyone has to start somewhere.

Jeremy Durst, of the Southern Oregon Jazz Orchestra, recommends you get out of your comfort zone and play in different locations to prepare for an audition. He said, "You need to be confident when auditioning and confidence comes with knowing you are not going to make a mistake." If you want to be in a band, "You need to practice. Be over prepared. And be willing to take criticism."

DID YOU KNOW?!

The type of music you play determines which instruments you need. Every band will benefit from a drum, bass, guitar or keys. Add some horns and you'll create a whole new sound. Most bands benefit from a talented vocalist.

RULES AND ROLES

Once you've formed your band, you'll need to decide when and where practices will be held and what type of music your band will play. Assigning a band leader will help with this process. A good band leader doesn't make all the band's decisions but instead acts as a mediator when it comes to making decisions and **resolving** conflicts. Roles should be assigned to all band members to help **distribute** the workload and provide equity among the group.

BAND ROLES TO ASSIGN

SCHEDULER: Schedules practices, gigs, and keeps track of dates.

PROMOTER: Promotes the band and does the marketing.

BOOKKEEPER: Keeps track of finances.

ARRANGER: Arranges the music.

EQUIPMENT MANAGER: Looks after and cares for the equipment.

01 JANUARY

SUN	MON	TUE	WED	THU	FRI	SAT
31	1	BAND PRACTICE 2	3	BAND PRACTICE 4	5	BAND PRACTICE 6
7	8	9	BAND PRACTICE 10	11	12	BAND PRACTICE 13
14	BAND PRACTICE 15	16	17	BAND PRACTICE 18	19	PLAY @ RANDY'S PARTY!
21	22	BAND PRACTICE 23	24	BAND PRACTICE 25	26	27
28	BAND PRACTICE 29	30	BAND PRACTICE 31	1	2	3
4	5	6	7	8	9	10

Every band needs a place to rehearse. Many bands start out practicing in a band member's garage.

JOINING A BAND

If putting together your own band feels overwhelming, consider joining a band that already exists. Search for **auditions** locally—check your favorite hangouts and local newspapers for opportunities. Search online and ask around. Remember, when you go to an audition, you are choosing the band as much as they are choosing you.

THINK ABOUT IT

Before making any decisions about joining a band, consider these things:
Does this band fit your style?
Do they seem organized?
Are they professional?
Do you think you can get along with all the band members?

TIME TO TAKE IT ON THE ROAD

Once you've had plenty of practice and feel ready, it's time to perform for a live audience. Consider making your first performance free. People are more likely to try out a new band when it doesn't cost them anything. Don't be discouraged if the turnout is small. The more you perform, the more fans you will gain. You'll be playing for larger audiences in no time.

A house party is a great place to **debut** your band. A backyard performance can be a lot of fun with minimal stress. Pay attention to your audience and notice which songs they respond well to and which songs have them heading for the snacks.

BE A GOOD NEIGHBOR

Be considerate to your neighbors when you're practicing. Honor your town's designated quiet hours. Let neighbors know ahead of time when you have a practice or performance scheduled. Establishing good neighbor relationships is another way to gain fans.

One way to find more gigs is by word of mouth. Ask other bands that play similar music for suggestions. Think outside the box when searching for gigs.

If your band is planning a street performance, make sure to check with your local government first. Some towns require that you have a permit.

VENUE IDEAS FOR NEW BANDS

- Perform at house parties and work parties.
- Play for nonprofit organizations.
- Suggest your band take part in grand opening celebrations.
- See if you can provide background music at your favorite restaurants.
- Offer to play for college filmmakers and theater students.

WHAT HAPPENS IF YOU GET SICK?

Sometimes a band member will need a substitute. Keep a list of Backup players and their phone numbers. Most musicians are good about covering for one another. This is another reason why it's important to make friends in the industry.

READY, SET, RECORD

After you've been performing live, know a variety of songs, and can play them to perfection, it's time to record a demo. Renting studio space is expensive but offers a high-quality, professional sound. If you decide to record in a studio, make sure you are well prepared.

Sometimes a studio recording is not in the budget. Luckily, many places offer quality home recording equipment for rent. Do the best with what you have access to and your talents will prevail.

HOW TO HAVE A SUCCESSFUL STUDIO RECORDING
- Arrive early.
- Bring extras of everything (examples include: strings, picks, reeds, cords).
- Have a plan.
- Be professional.
- Leave the drama at home.

INCREASING YOUR FAN BASE

Once you have a demo, distribute it to venues that reflect the type of music you play. People love free things, so if it's in your band's budget, create some merchandise with your band's logo to give away.

Promoting your band can **consume** a lot of time and money. Set a schedule and a budget and stick to them. Don't underestimate the importance of making friends in the business. Word of mouth goes a

long way. Upload your music online. Create a website. There are many websites available for low cost or free. Your website doesn't need to be fancy, but it should look professional and provide a place where people can watch clips of your performances. Include links to buy your music and don't forget to ask for reviews. Positive reviews will help grow your fan base.

POPULAR PLACES TO UPLOAD AND SHARE YOUR MUSIC INCLUDE:
SOUNDCLOUD: The world's leading musical platform.
ITUNES: The largest musical retailer in America developed by Apple.
SPOTIFY: A music streaming service with worldwide access.
YOUTUBE: The most popular video sharing site online.
GOOGLE PLAY: Like iTunes but for Android users.

RANDY SCHERER IS A COMMERCIAL TRUMPET PLAYER, WHICH MEANS HE IS CONTRACTED TO PLAY ALL STYLES OF MUSIC. RANDY HAS SPENT HIS LIFE PLAYING IN **VARIOUS** BANDS. HE'S TRAVELED THE WORLD PLAYING ON CRUISE SHIPS, AND HE SPENT SEVERAL YEARS PLAYING FOR THE UNITED STATES AIR FORCE BAND. RANDY SAID, "IT'S IMPORTANT TO PRACTICE EVERY DAY. ALSO, LISTEN TO THE TYPE OF MUSIC YOU WANT TO PLAY. LEARN FROM THE BEST." IF YOU WANT TO BE IN A BAND, "PRACTICE. BE METHODICAL IN YOUR PRACTICE. VALUE IT. GO TO COLLEGE. GET A TUTOR. BE THE BEST MUSICIAN YOU CAN BE RIGHT NOW. AND BE WELL-ROUNDED!"

CARING FOR YOUR INSTRUMENTS

- Clean your instruments regularly.
- Always carry them in their cases.
- Do not leave them where they can be exposed to weather.
- Wipe them down immediately after playing.
- Take them to a professional right away if you suspect something is wrong.

21

CAREER OPTIONS

If you enjoy traveling, consider working for a cruise ship band. You can travel the world in **luxury**, playing for guests on world-renowned cruise ships. Your evenings will be spent performing but most mornings and early afternoons are open for you to explore the ship and different ports.

Cruise ship musicians play everything from big bands to Broadway, top 40 to jazz. To perform with these talented musicians, you must be able to read music well and be prepared to play most anything.

Restaurant and club owners like to hire bands to liven the atmosphere and create a certain vibe. When patrons engage in the music, they often stay longer and spend more money.

If you prefer staying on land, you might be interested in playing for local restaurants. A contract with a restaurant or club can provide you with a steady schedule and income. You're likely to have mornings and afternoons off as many bands don't begin performing until later in the day.

Another option for the career-minded musician is joining a military band. Each branch of the U.S. military has its own band. Being in a military band provides opportunities to travel, perform at important ceremonies, march in parades, play in concerts, and perform for influential people.

FAST FACT
Military bands perform in ceremonies. They also perform to raise soldier morale.

DID YOU KNOW?!
The United States Military Academy, also known as West Point, has a band that started at about the time of the American Revolution.

The United States Air Force Band does not require its members to have a college degree (though most members do). Acceptance into the band is based solely on performance.

Have you ever thought about being in a marching band? The Disneyland Band in Anaheim, California and the Main Street Philharmonic in Walt Disney World's Magic Kingdom are both professional marching bands.

These hardworking bands are a big part of the Disney theme parks' attractions. Many theme parks hire bands to provide entertainment for their guests. If theme parks are your idea of fun, consider working for a theme park band.

FAST FACT
Marching bands evolved from military bands.

Some bands prefer not to have a set schedule. In this case, weddings, parties, churches, and festivals are great gigs for these hobby or part-time bands. Venues like these allow bands more flexibility with their schedules.

A wedding band sets the tone for the special event. They may also help keep guests informed about the event's activities.

Becoming a part of a successful band may take time. It takes a lot of practice and sometimes it takes a while to find the right mix of musicians to make a band click. With hard work, perseverance, and passion, you will find the band that's right for you.

GLOSSARY

auditions (aw-DISH-uhnz): the act of trying out for something

complementary (KAHM-pluh-mint-airy): combining in a way that enhances or emphasizes the qualities of each other or another

consequences (KON-suh-kwenss-ez): the results of someone's actions

consume (kuhn-SOOM): to use up

debut (DAY-byoo or day-BYOO): a person's first performance in front of an audience or their first release of something they created

distribute (diss-TRIB-yoot): to give or pass out

luxury (LUHK-shuh-ree or LUHG-zhuh-ree): a comfortable way of life, full of expensive things

maintain (mayn-TAYN): to continue something

resolving (ri-ZOLV-ing): to make an effort to do something

various (VAR-ee-uhss): several or different

INDEX

audience(s) 11, 13

concert(s) 24, 26

demo 16, 18

entertainment 27

fan(s) 4, 11, 13, 18, 19

gigs 8, 14, 28

music 4, 7, 8, 14, 18, 19, 20 22, 23

musician(s) 5, 9, 15, 20, 22, 24, 29

perform 11, 14, 22, 24, 26

practice(s) 7, 8, 11, 12, 13, 20, 29

record 16

songs 13, 16

studio 16

venue(s) 14, 18, 28

SHOW WHAT YOU KNOW

1. Why is it a good idea to have auditions?

2. Describe the role of a good band leader.

3. Where are some places you could look for auditions?

4. When will your band be ready to record?

5. Name some places where a new band could perform.

FURTHER READING

Owen, Ruth, *I Can Start a Band! (Kids Can Do It!)*, Windmill Books, 2017.

Gilpin, Daniel, *Start Your Own Band (Quick Expert's Guide)*, Rosen Publishing Group, 2014.

Saxena, Shalina, *Top 101 Musicians (People You Should Know)*, Britannica Publishing, 2014.

ABOUT THE AUTHOR

Michelle Garcia Andersen comes from a family of musicians. Although she does not play in a band, she goes to many band concerts for her son and daughter. Her brother and nieces are also very talented musicians.

Meet The Author!
www.meetREMauthors.com

www.rourkeeducationalmedia.com

PHOTO CREDITS: Cover & Title Pg ©DeshaCAM, Pg 7, 12, 20 ©MariatKary, Pg 4 ©RyanJLane, Pg 5 ©South_agency, Pg 6 ©solitude72, Pg 7 ©By Lilkin, ©Nerthuz, Pg 8 ©extracoin, Pg 9 ©trekandshoot, ©By Rawpixel.com, Pg 10 ©Vasyl Dolmatov, Pg 11 ©PeopleImages, Pg 12 ©Alison Hopkins, Pg 13 ©martin-dm, Pg 14 ©By Cebas, Pg 15 ©gpointstudio, ©koya79, Pg 17 ©SolStock, Pg 18 ©FlamingPumpkin, Pg 19 ©By A. Aleksandravicius, Pg 20 ©Jamie Luke, Pg 21 ©Maica, Pg 22 ©Ron S Buskirk/Alamy Stock Photo, Pg 23 ©Torontonian/Alamy Stock Photo, Pg 24 ©Ron S Buskirk/Alamy Stock Photo, Pg 26 ©Findlay/Alamy Stock Photo, Pg 28 ©By Siberia Video and Photo, Pg 29 ©ManuelVelasco

Edited by: Keli Sipperley
Cover and Interior design by: Rhea Magaro-Wallace

Library of Congress PCN Data

In a Band / Michelle Garcia Andersen
(So You Wanna Be)
ISBN 978-1-64156-471-7 (hard cover)
ISBN 978-1-64156-597-4 (soft cover)
ISBN 978-1-64156-712-1 (e-Book)
Library of Congress Control Number: 2018930507

Rourke Educational Media
Printed in the United States of America,
North Mankato, Minnesota